LIGHT

KAY DAVIES
AND
WENDY OLDFIELD

RSVP
RAINTREE
STECK-VAUGHN
PUBLISHERS
The Steck-Vaughn Company

Austin, Texas

Starting Science

Books in the series

About This Book

Information in **Light** is closely linked to practical activities dealing with this subject, so that children can learn from firsthand experience. Topics include how light is produced and how it is reflected and refracted. Children discover that light travels in straight lines and also how colors can be mixed. Investigations with color and pattern show their importance in the natural world and how they can play tricks on our eyes.

This book provides an introduction to methods in scientific inquiry and recording. The activities and investigations are designed to be straightforward but fun, and flexible according to the abilities of the children.

The main picture and its commentary may be taken as an introduction to the topic or as a focal point for further discussion. Each chapter can form a basis for extended topic work.

Teachers and parents will find that in using this book, they are reinforcing the other core subjects of language and mathematics. Through its topical approach **Light** covers aspects of the following subjects: exploration of science, the variety of life, types and uses of materials, and using light and electromagnetic radiation.

©Copyright this edition 1992
Steck-Vaughn Company

All rights reserved. No reproduction, copy, or transmission of this publication may be made without permission of the publisher.

Editors: Cally Chambers, Susan Wilson

Typeset by Multifacit Graphics, Keyport, NJ
Printed and bound in the U.S. by Lake Book, Melrose Park, IL

2 3 4 5 6 7 8 9 0 LB 96 95 94 93 92

**Library of Congress
Cataloging-in-Publication Data**

Davies, Kay.
  Light / written by Kay Davies and Wendy Oldfield.
    p.   cm. — (Starting science)
  Includes bibliographical references (p. 31) and index.
  Summary: Text, illustrations, and suggested activities introduce the properties, sources, and effects of light.

  1. Light — Juvenile literature. 2. Light — Experiments — Juvenile literature. [1. Light — Experiments. 2. Experiments.] I. Oldfield, Wendy. II. Title. III. Series: Davies, Kay. Starting science.
  QC360.D38 1992   91-30067
  535—dc20   CIP AC

ISBN 0-8114-3006-5 hardcover library binding
ISBN 0-8114-1530-9 softcover binding

CONTENTS

The words that first appear in **bold** in the text or captions are explained in the glossary.

Light comes from the sun and shines on the Earth.
The moon glows because it **reflects** the sun's light.

LIGHTING UP THE SKY

The sun is a star. Stars are very hot and give off light.

The Earth and moon do not give off light.

Light from the sun hits the Earth. Light can reflect, or bounce off, things. We see things because they reflect light.

We also see things that give off their own light. This happens when something burns or gets really hot. Look at these things.

Sort them into two groups.
1. Those that make their own light when they get hot.
2. Those that have no light of their own but only reflect light.

BRIGHT EYES

We can only see a small part of the eye. The eye is round like a ball and is kept safe inside the head.

We can see the colored iris and dark pupil.

The pupil is an opening that lets light shine into your eye.

Bright light makes the pupil get smaller. This stops too much light from getting in.

In the dark, the pupil opens wide to let in extra light so we can see better.

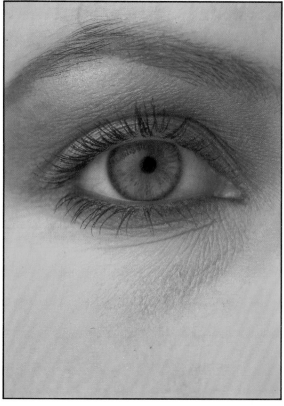

Look at your friend's eyes.

How big are the pupils?

Now shine a dim flashlight in your friend's eyes.

What happened to the pupils?

It isn't easy to see in the dark forest at night.
The bushbaby has huge eyes to catch lots of light.

MIRROR MONSTERS

When light bounces off shiny things it makes a **reflection**. A reflection is an **image** that we can see.

Mirrors that are flat give the best reflections.

Curved mirrors can make things look bigger, smaller, or change their shape. They can even turn things upside down.

Try looking at your face in the front of a spoon and then the back.

Look at your reflection in a shiny car. What do you notice?

Look around your home and school for other things that make reflections.

Make a collection of shiny things that reflect light.

What are they made of?

Wavy mirrors twist and bend shapes.
We can see ourselves, but we look like strange monsters.

The flat surface of the lake is like a mirror.
Turn the picture upside down. Does it look the same?

MIRROR IMAGE

If you look in a mirror you see a reflection of yourself.

This is your image.

Raise your right hand.

Does your image do the same?

Wink your left eye. Watch what your image does.

How is your image different from you?

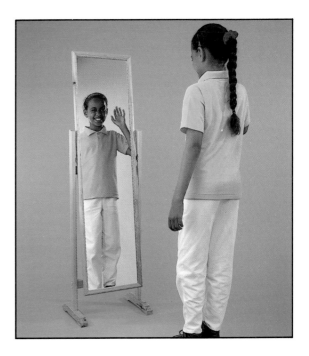

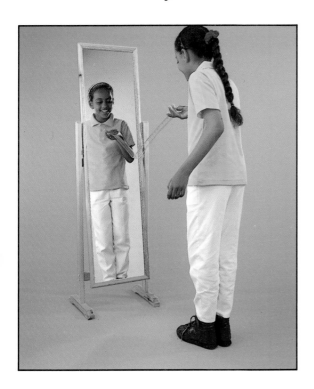

Touch the surface of the mirror with the end of a ruler.

How far away from the mirror is your hand?

How far away from the mirror is your image's hand?

Where do you think the image really is?

BOUNCING AROUND

Mirrors can help you play tricks with light.

Hold a mirror on a broken line. Move it to the other lines. How many bears can you see each time?

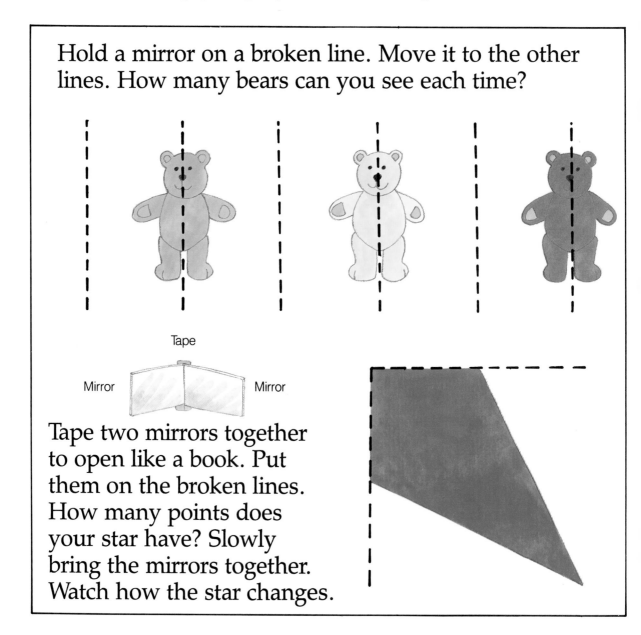

Tape two mirrors together to open like a book. Put them on the broken lines. How many points does your star have? Slowly bring the mirrors together. Watch how the star changes.

You can make a **kaleidoscope** from three small mirrors. Tape them together to make a triangle. Drop paper shapes inside. Look into the corners to see your patterns.

Light bounces between the mirrors in a kaleidoscope.
It turns a handful of shapes into a beautiful pattern.

In strong light, shadows follow us everywhere.
They stand in our shoes and copy everything we do.

ME AND MY SHADOW

Light always travels in straight lines. It cannot bend around things.

When an object blocks the light's path, dark shapes, called shadows, appear.

Use your hands to make some shadow shapes on the wall.

You will need a bright light behind you.

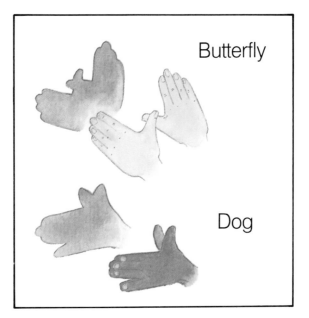

Butterfly

Dog

Use lots of things to make shadows. Move them about.

Do the shadows change shape as you move the objects?

Play a shadow guessing game with your friends.

Can they tell what makes each shadow?

The sun shines through the mist and makes a rainbow.
Do you know the colors? Are they always the same?

SUNSHINE THROUGH RAIN

Things that we can easily see through are **transparent**.

Air, water, and glass are all transparent. Light can pass through them. Can you find anything transparent?

Usually the light from the sun or a lamp looks white. Light that looks white is really a mixture of many colors.

If sunlight shines through rain or mist, these colors can make a rainbow.

Glass, like this **prism**, can make a rainbow too.

Look at the picture. How many colors can you find?

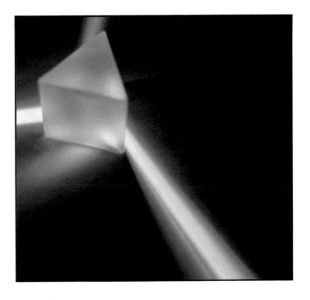

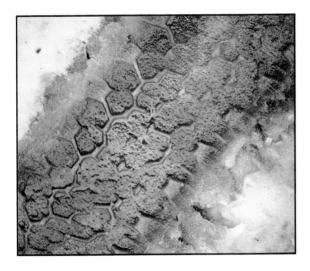

Look for colors in puddles and at the edges of mirrors, jewelry, **cut glass**, and fish tanks.

Blow some bubbles. Can you see a rainbow in them?

MIX AND MATCH

Put clean water in a jar.

Add a few drops of red paint to the water.

Add some drops of blue paint to the water.

What color can you see where the paints mix? Have you made a new color?

Paint a color wheel.

Paint three slices with just one color — red, yellow, and blue.

Mix two colors together for the in-between slices.

Can you name the new colors you have made?

What happens if you mix all three paints together?

The artist is painting a picture. He mixes paints together
to make many different colors.

The window is made of colored glass. The sun shines through and makes patterns of light on the floor.

CHANGING COLORS

Colored light can make things look different.

Make a peephole in one end of a shoe box.

Make a larger hole in the lid. Cover this hole with a **colored filter**.

Put different colored objects inside the box.

Hold the box in bright light and look through the peephole.

Try different color filters.

How do the colors in the box change each time?

Make a chart of what you see.

Color of light filter	Red objects looked:	Green objects looked:	Blue objects looked:	Yellow objects looked:
Red Green Blue Yellow	Red	Black	Purple	Orange

The insect looks like the leaves it lives on. It is the same shape and color. It can only be seen when it moves.

WHERE AM I?

Many animals have colors and patterns that make them hard to see. They are **camouflaged**.

Their coloring and patterns look like the plants or the land on which they live. This helps the animals hide from others that might harm them.

Can you find the animals hidden in this picture?

Make some snakes. Make some brightly colored. Color the others green, black, and brown. Tape them to a background of grass and trees. Which are hardest to see?

I'M WARNING YOU!

Some pairs of colors really stand out.

Many **poisonous** animals and plants use these colors. They warn other animals to leave them alone.

Make some colored cards like these. Stick different colored crosses on these backgrounds.

Make sure they are all the same size.

Tape all the cards to the wall.

Ask your friends to stand at the other side of the room.

Ask them which card they find easiest to see.

Make a picture graph to show your results.

The wasp doesn't need to hide. Its black and yellow bands warn other animals that it is dangerous.

Familiar objects look strange in close-up pictures.
Can you guess what this is? You might like to eat it.

CLOSE-UP

Lenses are specially shaped pieces of glass or plastic. Some bulge out and some curve in. They bend the light.

A **magnifying glass** is a lens. Both sides of the lens bulge out.

Use a magnifying glass to look at objects around you. You might notice things you don't usually see.

Make your own lens.

Spread a piece of plastic wrap over a roll of tape. Drop a little water on the plastic wrap.

Hold your lens over words in a newspaper.

Try adding more water and gently stretching the plastic wrap to find the best magnifying glass.

PLAYING TRICKS

Things aren't always what they seem. Strong colors and patterns of lines can fool your eyes.

Look at the picture below. The bricklayers have built a wall with black and white bricks. Have they laid them straight? Use a ruler to check.

Moving pictures trick us too. Make a little book. Start at the back and copy the drawings in order. Draw each one on a fresh page near the edge. Flick through the pages from back to front with your thumb. Can you see the person jumping?

Hot air rises from the baking desert.
It can play tricks with the light and we see **mirages**.

GLOSSARY

Camouflaged An animal is camouflaged when it is difficult to see because its coloring and pattern look like its surroundings.

Color filter Transparent plastic or glass that only lets through light of the same color as the filter.

Cut glass A kind of glass that has patterns cut into it.

Image The copy of something we see when we look in a mirror or other shiny surface.

Kaleidoscope A collection of mirrors that bounce light between them to make colorful patterns.

Lenses Pieces of transparent material with curved surfaces that change the direction of the light.

Magnifying glass A lens that makes objects look bigger.

Mirage An image of water which isn't really there.

Poisonous Animals and plants are poisonous if, by their bite or by being eaten, they cause illness or death to other animals.

Prism A transparent triangle shape that can separate white light into rainbow colors.

Reflect To bounce light back off an object.

Reflection The image we see reflected in a shiny surface.

Transparent Materials like glass or plastic, which let light pass through. We can see through transparent objects.

FINDING OUT MORE

Books to read:

Experiments with Light by R. Broekel, "New True Books" series
   (Childrens Press, 1986)
Heat, Lights and Action! How Electricity Works by Eve and Albert Stwertka
   (Silver Burdett Press, 1991)
Light by Rae Bains (Troll Assocs., 1985)
Light by Brenda Walpole (Franklin Watts, 1987)
Light by Angela Webb (Franklin Watts, 1988)
Light and Color by L.W. Anderson (Raintree Pubs., 1987)
Light and Color by Terry Jennings, "The Young Scientist Investigates" series
   (Childrens Press)
Mirrors by Julie Fitzpatrick (Silver Burdett Press)
Simple Science Experiments with Light by Eiji and Masako Orii
   (Gareth Stevens, 1989)
Your Eyes by Joan Iveson-Iveson (Franklin Watts, 1986)

PICTURE ACKNOWLEDGMENTS

Chris Fairclough Colour Library 19; Eye Ubiquitous 13; Hutchison 4; PHOTRI 26;
Tony Stone Worldwide 10, 14, 16, 17 both; Wayland Picture Library 9, (Zul
Mukhida) cover, 6 bottom, 8, 11 both, 15, 18 both, 21, 24, 27 both; ZEFA 6 top, 7,
20, 22, 25, 29.
Artwork illustrations by Rebecca Archer. Cover design by Angela Hicks.

INDEX

First published in 1990 by Wayland
(Publishers) Ltd.
©Copyright 1990 Wayland (Publishers) Ltd.